Original title:
A Home Filled with Green

Copyright © 2025 Creative Arts Management OÜ
All rights reserved.

Author: Sebastian Whitmore
ISBN HARDBACK: 978-1-80581-854-0
ISBN PAPERBACK: 978-1-80581-381-1
ISBN EBOOK: 978-1-80581-854-0

Dew-kissed Moments of Stillness

In a house where the ferns tend to dance,
The sunlight winks, giving plants a chance.
Sassy succulents roll their eyes,
While sleeping cacti dream of pies.

Pansies giggle in cheerful beds,
As wandering weeds form silly threads.
The ivy whispers jokes in the night,
Tickling the walls with leafy delight.

Sanctuary of Chlorophyll Kisses

There's a pea pod dressed in tiny shoes,
Stirring up chaos while sipping its blues.
Spinach sits smirking, full of sass,
While radishes hold an underground class.

The herb brigade plots their green schemes,
To win the garden in sunny dreams.
Basil cracks jokes, oh what a thrill,
While rosemary rolls with a perfumed chill.

Harmonies in Leafy Dreams

In a corner, a fern plays the sax,
While daisies tap dance, avoiding the tax.
The orchids are blushing, oh what a sight,
As fuchsia finds fame with her bright, bold light.

Cactus beats drums in a prickly way,
Reviving old plants for a party today.
Lavender giggles, tuning her voice,
With thyme at the helm, oh what a choice!

The Symbiosis of Roots and Reverie

A sunflower grins, tall and so proud,
While daisies gossip, eager and loud.
Beanstalks are stretching, reaching for skies,
Conspiring with clouds, in clever disguise.

Lettuce plays low, hiding its grin,
While carrots compete, trying to win.
The garden hums with nature's own beat,
As worms waltz below in their earthy retreat.

The Aroma of Earth

In the corner, sprouts abound,
Cabbage sings a silly sound.
Tomatoes juggling on the vine,
Dancing squash, oh how divine!

Compost piles, they start to hum,
Worms are grooving, here they come!
Garlic breath wafts through the air,
Even rabbits stop and stare.

Sheltered by Green Canopies

Under leaves the shadows play,
Squirrels dare to wrestle, hey!
A toad croaks jokes with delight,
While frogs splash in a water fight.

Tall branches bend to share a tease,
Breezes whisper, 'Do as you please!'
A chicken struts with froggy flair,
And grasshoppers simply stare.

Nature's Gentle Refuge

In the garden, gnomes conspire,
Spilling secrets by the fire.
Ladybugs play hide and seek,
While chubby bunnies munch a leek.

Ants put on a marching show,
Frogs hop wide, aiming low.
A flower tripped and took a fall,
But smiled bright, oh what a ball!

Verdant Horizons

Kites caught in a leafy snare,
As wind plays tag without a care.
Pickles giggle in jars so tight,
While pickers dance with pure delight.

Pinecones tumble, gathering dust,
In antics that we all must trust.
Sunflowers nod with laughter free,
As nature sings, 'Come dance with me!'

Garden of Serenity

In the yard, a gnome stood tall,
Holding up his tiny sprawl.
Flowers giggle as they bloom,
Making sure the weeds find room.

Butterflies wear silly hats,
Chasing bees with all the spats.
Rain drops skip from leaf to leaf,
As puddles laugh in sheer belief.

Where Ferns Dance

Ferns wear tutus, light and bright,
Swaying gently, what a sight!
Critters join a waltz of cheer,
While squirrels play the tambourine here.

A worm breaks out into a jig,
Making all the spiders gig.
Nature's friendly, kooky spree,
Dancing under the old oak tree.

The Heart of Nature

Roots tickle grass beneath the ground,
Making giggles, oh so profound.
Trees whisper secrets to the breeze,
While ants perform their choreographed tease.

Sunlight sprinkles like confetti,
As squirrels paint the world all sweaty.
A frog jumps in, splashes so wide,
Just another day with nature as a guide.

Blossoms in the Breeze

Blossoms wiggle, dance with flair,
Sending pollen everywhere!
The daisies plot a game of tag,
While tulips wear a sassy rag.

Dandelions float like fluff,
Sharing wishes, oh so tough.
It's a party, come and see,
Where laughter blooms so carelessly!

Nature's Secret Nook

In a corner, plants wear hats,
Potted succulents chatting with cats.
Ferns gossip about the sun's glare,
While cacti claim they don't have a care.

Basil thinks it's a chef's best friend,
But rosemary says it's all just pretend.
The bonsai tree, all trimmed so neat,
Mumbles, 'Gossip over, let's eat!'

A Tapestry of Wild Green

The ivy climbed with such great flair,
It tangled up the neighbor's hair.
Moss made a couch that seemed so grand,
But frogs claimed it as their own land.

Pansies giggled at bees in a tizz,
Saying, 'Honey, you're quite the whiz!'
Gardening gloves waged a soft war,
On who gets to hug the earth once more.

Sunlight Dancing on Dusty Windows

Sunbeams waltz on panes so bright,
While dust bunnies giggle in morning light.
A spider spins, with threads of gold,
Whispering secrets that never get old.

Moths might have crash courses at night,
While curtains sway like they're in flight.
The dog snores loud, dreams of a bone,
Wakes up startled, but still feels at home.

The Dance of Shadows in Foliage

Shadows frolic under leafy cover,
Chasing each other like a playful lover.
Squirrels plot mischief in the trees,
While woodpeckers practice their parties with ease.

Laughter echoes through leafy lanes,
As sunflowers wink at the passing trains.
The wind joins in with a cheeky cheer,
Whispering secrets for all to hear.

Paths of Growth through Chambered Memory

In a corner, a plant sits snug,
Wearing a hat that's way too big.
It winks at the cactus with a shrug,
Together, they dance, a funny jig.

The garden gnome looks on in awe,
With his mismatched shoes and silly grin.
He spills the soil, oh what a flaw,
But the flowers giggle, letting him in.

Vines creep up the wall with glee,
Whispering secrets to the old bookshelf.
Each leaf holds a tale of mystery,
As if they're laughing at the shelf's self.

In the bathtub, a fern declares,
"This is a spa for dirt and delight!"
Rub-a-dub with soapy airs,
It's the silliest sight, oh what a sight!

The Joy of Sprouting Spaces

Tiny sprouts burst from their beds,
Peeking out with curious eyes.
They giggle softly, toss their heads,
As the sun teases, brightening the skies.

A rogue potato tries to dance,
Rolling over with a funny flair.
In this garden, there's a chance,
To join in laughter and fresh air.

Butterflies join the merry band,
Twirling 'round, they shake and fold.
Even the rocks have joined the stand,
With their stone faces, stories told.

Every leaf is a burst of cheer,
Tickling the breeze with their charming grace.
Life's a party all year,
In this sprouting, giggly space!

Vibrant Canopy

In corners, plants do dance and sway,
Cacti wear hats, it's their big day.
Pothos plays peek-a-boo with the light,
While ferns gossip softly about their height.

Basil believes it's a culinary king,
As thyme tries to charm with its zing.
Fake plants cackle, saying they're blessed,
While we water friends who just need a rest.

The Green Tapestry

My plants have formed a leafy crew,
Plotting a garden takeover, too.
Sage readies a joke about the sun,
But mint just yawns, says, 'We've just begun!'

In the corner, a fern's so bold,
Wearing a scarf, a sight to behold.
The dracaena sings out, 'Not so loud!'
While succulents giggle, feeling so proud.

Oasis of Tranquility

The rubber plant thinks it's a celebrity,
With selfies taken, oh, such brevity.
A snake plant claims to be a star,
'Just look at me, I've come so far!'

Lettuce whispers secrets in the soil,
While daisies laugh, stripped of all toil.
But the peace lily says with a bright grin,
'At least we're not drowning in sin!'

House of Leaves

A leafy cottage full of cheer,
Where vines dangle, near and dear.
The pots joke with roots all intertwined,
'At least we're not left behind!'

In the warmth, the green party thrives,
While basil dreams of pizza dives.
Moss is the guest that never leaves,
In this room bursting with planty thieves.

Emerald Embrace

In the corner, a plant took a dive,
Its leaves flapping, oh, it's alive!
The cat thinks it's a friendly foe,
Together they wrestle, putting on a show.

The cactus wears a tiny hat,
Thinking it's tough, but look at that!
With a sip of sun, it struts around,
While wondering why it can't be found.

The fern has dreams of traveling far,
Wants to hitch a ride in a toy car!
Each leaf whispers, "Oh, what a thrill!"
But here it stays, all green and still.

Dancing shadows, a plant parade,
The orchids giggle, the sun's their aide.
With every sprout, the laughter streams,
A jungle of joy, where nature dreams.

Verdant Whispers

In the kitchen, herbs plot and scheme,
Basil whispers, "Let's start a dream!"
Thyme rolls its eyes, "Not another plan,
Last time you tried, you burned the pan."

The aloe's grumpy, "Why am I here?
I just wanna sip on some cold root beer!"
But every time they gather round,
The funniest mayhem can be found.

Potted friends like to tell tall tales,
About adventures on windy trails.
"Yesterday, I saw a giant bug!"
"Don't be silly, it was just a rug!"

Laughter echoes, leaves catch the sound,
In this funny patch, joy is abound.
When sunlight spills and shadows dance,
The chatter grows, each green leaf's prance!

The Lush Haven

The ficus wears a sparkly gown,
Swaying gently while looking down.
It says, "With every twist and turn,
I'm still the best, just wait and learn!"

The pothos tries to climb the wall,
But gets tangled, taking a fall.
"Help me, friends!" it calls with flair,
"Next time I'll wear sensible hair!"

Moss giggles softly on the floor,
"When will those vines stop keeping score?"
Each branch has dreams that will not quit,
In laughter's glow, they choose to sit.

With every gurgle of watering can,
A symphony starts, a plant-filled band.
They sway and croon, a leafy song,
In their lush haven, where joy belongs.

Leafy Sanctuary

In the middle of the room, what a sight,
A jungle of joy, a pure delight.
The monkey grass giggles, "Look at me!"
"I'm the fastest sprout; just wait and see!"

The geraniums gossip, with petals so bold,
"Did you hear about the marigold?"
"She wore too much fertilizer last week,
Now she's shy and refuses to speak!"

The succulents sit, with arms crossed tight,
"Too much drama, we'll leave tonight!"
But they stay for the party, with drinks so sweet,
In their leafy sanctuary, they dance on their feet.

When the moonlight spills and shadows play,
Plant pals giggle, what a lovely day.
In every corner, green joy beams,
Their quirky world fulfills all dreams!

Ferns and Fables

In a nook where ferns dance,
Silly gnomes do prance.
Chasing bugs in silly hats,
Laughing with the chatty cats.

Socks that vanish in the shade,
Worms invite a grand charade.
Telling tales of shades and light,
Each leaf whispers, 'What a sight!'

Cucumbers wear a leafy crown,
Carrots tiptoe through the town.
Where will all the veggies go?
A mystery that makes us glow!

Sunlight tickles every stem,
A chorus sung by every gem.
Plants hold secrets, oh so sly,
While mushrooms giggle, oh my my!

A Canvas of Nature

Painted pots in dazzling hues,
Flowers wear their Sunday shoes.
Bees make music on their flight,
Buzzing tunes both day and night.

Pansies throw a wild party,
Inviting butterflies so hearty.
Tulips dressed in polka dots,
Sing with laughter, lots and lots.

When rain begins, it feels like play,
The seedlings jump and sway away.
A garden dance, all in line,
Sprouting joy, oh how divine!

The sun, a jester in the sky,
Tickling clouds as they float by.
In this realm of blooms so grand,
Laughter grows across the land!

Where Vines Intertwine

Vines are tangled, what a mess,
A loving knot, or just distress?
Swaying like a raucous band,
Strumming leaves across the land.

A snail's race, will he win this time?
With every slide, he thinks he's prime.
While frogs critique his speedy flair,
They laugh and leap without a care.

Tomatoes wear their finest gowns,
Giggles echo through the towns.
Zucchini dances in the breeze,
Chortling sweetly with such ease.

In the midst of leafy cheer,
Squirrels peek from far and near.
When the kitchen calls dessert,
Basil grins; it's time to flirt!

The Breath of Botany

In the air, a minty trace,
Leaves turn green with such pure grace.
A dance of thyme, a jig of dill,
Laughter floats; it's quite the thrill.

Parsley sneezes, 'Oh, not again!'
While chives giggle; they love the pen.
Herbs throw parties under the sun,
Each leaf partakes; they're all in fun.

A cactus jokes, "Prick me, no way!"
While sunflowers nod, 'We're here to stay!'
In pots and plots, the laughter brews,
With every heart that nature woos.

Blooms and shrubs, they share their dreams,
And giggle softly at life's schemes.
For in this patch, where green things dwell,
Joy sprouts up; it casts its spell!

The Echo of Forests

In the woods, a squirrel danced,
Chasing shadows, he pranced.
Barked at trees, quite out of tune,
Claimed the night, beneath the moon.

Frogs croaked jokes from the marsh,
While birds chirped in a harsh quash.
A raccoon tried to sing a song,
But the crickets called it wrong.

Leaves giggled, high up they shook,
Twirling round like a storybook.
The owls hooted, 'What a sight!'
Nighttime jesters of delight.

Nature's laughter, wild and free,
In the heart of the tall pine tree.
Echoes bounce in bright banter,
Every laugh, a joyous canter.

Nestled in Greenery

Under branches, a cat naps deep,
While the flowers gossip, never sleep.
Bees wear sweaters, striped with pride,
As butterflies show off, they glide.

A turtle waddles, quite a sight,
In slow motion, he takes flight.
Snails race past with great flails,
Claiming victory, leaving trails.

Rabbits argue, 'Who's the best?
The one with the biggest nest?'
While hedgehogs roll into a ball,
Sharing secrets, big and small.

In this patch, so much cheer,
Nature's circus, come and near.
With giggles sprouting everywhere,
Who knew green could be such flair?

Whispering Leaves

Leaves confide in the soft breeze,
'Can you believe the fuss with trees?'
Giggles echo through the air,
As sunlight gives the shade a glare.

Breezes poke at the ferns so shy,
'Wanna play hide and seek?' they cry.
But the bushes just shake their heads,
Hiding secrets, snug in beds.

A dragonfly dons a tiny hat,
As ants argue who's first, the brat.
In giggly sways, branches jive,
With every turn, they feel alive.

The whispers weave a playful tale,
Of creatures small who never fail.
Each rustle brings another jest,
In this forest, laughter's best!

Treetop Fantasies

On a branch, a squirrel jokes,
Passing clouds, he pokes and prods.
'Think you're fluffy? Check this out!'
He leaps, spins, gives a shout.

The owls wear glasses quite askew,
Reading books on subjects new.
'This page says cats chase their tails,'
While the mice pipe in, 'No fails!'

Raccoons play cards beneath the stars,
As fireflies hum like tiny cars.
They stack their chips— acorns galore,
Who knew nighttime could hold such roar?

Every branch is a stage for glee,
With humor sprouting like a tree.
In this lofty whimsical game,
It's all about who's got the name!

Nature's Gentle Breath

Leaves dance lightly, a wobbly jig,
Squirrels debate, who's the dance king?
The flowers giggle, they can't hold in,
While snails argue who'll finish the sprint.

A cactus snickers, it wears a crown,
While ferns sway softly, not wearing a frown.
Laughter erupts from a bold bumblebee,
Buzzing a tune of wild jubilee.

The oak pretends to be taller than tall,
While daisies chuckle, they feel quite small.
A breeze whispers secrets, so light and spry,
Cheerful chaos under an open sky.

Rooted in mischief, the garden's alive,
With veggies plotting a garden-wide jive.
Lettuce is laughing, as tomatoes hug tight,
In this green playground, everything's light.

Roots of Comfort

Under the soil, the jokes take root,
Worms share puns, in their little suit.
The onions cry, but it's all for fun,
While radishes giggle, 'We've just begun.'

Potatoes hide, they think it's a game,
'Let's play rock, paper, scissors!' they claim.
Moss cushions laughter, so fluffy and warm,
In this cozy patch, there's quite the charm.

Bees play tag with a butterfly fleet,
As daisies burst forth in a dance so sweet.
Roots intertwine, they all want a say,
In this rooty comedy, where laughter holds sway.

In this green haven, where tickles abound,
Each plant is a joker, each leaf makes a sound.
The soil's tickled pink, with jokes that it keeps,
While the garden chuckles, as the whole world sleeps.

Symphony of Chlorophyll

Grass sings softly, a whispering tune,
Leaves clap along, under a bright moon.
The sunflowers sway, with a hippy's flair,
While crickets provide a metronome air.

The mossy rocks join in, fortified cheer,
As dandelions toss their fluff without fear.
A frog leaps high, jazz hands in the air,
The lily pad floats with comedian flair.

A raccoon strums branches, too cool for class,
While rabbits join roundups, and let moments pass.
Nature's orchestra, full of surprises,
With rustling leaves as the giggling prizes.

In this concert hall, every note shines bright,
A melody crafted from day into night.
With laughter as rhythm, the world spins around,
In verdant vibes, joy and warmth abound.

Sanctuary Among the Sycamores

In the shade of giants, giggles abound,
Where branch and bark seem to dance all around.
The acorns tumble, they roll and they race,
While chipmunks play tag, in nature's embrace.

The breeze blows softly, it tickles the leaves,
As spiders weave webs that nobody sees.
The groundhog pops out, wearing a grin,
He shimmies and shakes, it's a win-win-win!

The owls hoot jokes from their leafy retreats,
As squirrels perform acrobatical feats.
A sanctuary lively, where laughter prevails,
With each little critter sharing tall tales.

Under the sycamores, all hearts feel light,
Where joy is the sunshine that chases the night.
In this leafy refuge, full of surprise,
Life's one big joke, wrapped in nature's guise.

The Quiet Arboretum

In the garden, plants have a chat,
With the squirrels wearing tiny hats.
The daisies gossip, oh so bold,
While the ferns try to keep it controlled.

A sunflower's joke goes right over heads,
The tulips laugh till the soil sheds.
A scarecrow feels quite out of place,
With a carrot looking him square in the face.

The wind whispers secrets, only they know,
As the moles practice their stand-up show.
Beneath the treetops, life's quite absurd,
The puns from the bunnies are truly unheard.

So let's gather near, for a giggle and cheer,
Where the green leaves dance, and no one's austere.
Nature's comedy club is in full swing,
And the laughter of petals makes the heart sing.

The Enchanted Canopy

Up in the branches, the secrets spill,
As parrots argue over their meal.
Branches dance in a marvelous twist,
While the chubby chipmunks can't help but exist.

A raccoon wearing a leaf for a tie,
Sings to the moon with a wink in his eye.
The vines weave stories of days gone by,
While the sleepy sloth just yawns and sighs.

Laughter echoes in the cool afternoon,
As bees hum along like a funny tune.
The saplings play tag, so spryly and spry,
While the wise old owl just rolls on by.

In this leafy lounge, all ponder and dream,
While sparks of humor create quite the scheme.
So grab a twig, let's make a scene,
In this delightful play of shades and green.

Memories Among the Green

In the thicket where laughter entwines,
The lettuce recounts ancient lines.
Cabbages gossip with mischievous flair,
While the carrots joke about dating a hare.

The daisies prance in ballet so sweet,
Telling stories of whom they might meet.
A rogue acorn trips on a twig,
Causing a tumble so hilariously big.

Pine needles chuckle, oh what a tease,
While the lilacs giggle in the cool breeze.
Old oaks reminisce of a time long past,
When squirrels were grandmasters, oh how they'd blast!

Gather round, in this theater of green,
Where the humor is bright and the air is serene.
These memories dance between each leaf,
In this quirky patch of joyful relief.

Serenity in Leaves

Oh, the leaves whisper tales of yore,
About critters who danced and maybe more.
The branches chuckle, swaying with glee,
As the petals gossip like tea over tea.

The sunbeams tickle the daisies' faces,
While butterflies float to mysterious places.
A hedgehog reads poems to passing toes,
Sharing tales of the thorns and the posies' woes.

In the shade, cucumbers crack silly jokes,
While the radish outruns the old, wise folks.
Morning glories giggle, blooming so bright,
In this peaceful realm, humor takes flight.

With every rustle, a punchline is made,
In this garden of laughs where worries fade.
So sit back, relax, let your heart take a tease,
In this oasis of joy, serenity in leaves.

The Abode of Growth

In the living room, a sprout does wiggle,
It thinks it's a pet, but makes me giggle.
The cat gives chase, leaps over the chair,
Yet the plant stays still, just without a care.

A fern on the shelf, doing some yoga,
Stretched and flexible, it's quite the doga.
The sunbeam hits just right on its leaves,
What a way to shine, oh how it believes!

A cactus in the corner wears a straw hat,
Thinking it's cool, like a petting cat.
The guests all laugh, say it's quite the sight,
A prickly friend joining in on the light.

The pots all chat, a leafy affair,
Each swapping tales of who grows where.
While the roots underneath engage in a dance,
In this house of green, who needs romance?

Soft Mossy Corners

In every nook where the sunlight sneaks,
Moss grows thick, as if it speaks.
It cushions my feet, a soft, green rug,
But when I trip, oh what a bug!

The couch is live with creeping vines,
They've made the cushions their climbing lines.
I sit down, they give a playful tug,
Do I need to rescue my own snug bug?

The corner's now home to a bold little sprout,
Bounced by the cat, there's never a doubt.
It dances with joy, thinks it's a star,
While the dusty old books laugh from afar.

Soft moss days turn into leafy nights,
With shadows playing and silly sights.
In the corners where green makes a mess,
Life's a grand joke, and I must confess!

Sheltered by Nature

Under the roof where the green life dwells,
The ivy climbs up, casting leafy spells.
It whispers sweet nothings to the wall,
While I trip over pots—every time I fall.

The windows are dressed in a leafy crown,
Birds peek in, then quickly bounce down.
They chirp and chat, with their feathery grace,
While I sip my tea, just trying to brace.

A rabbit hops by, it's eating the prize,
Dandelions sprout, to my great surprise.
I've built a garden, but it seems they've won,
Next year I'll join them, oh what fun!

Surrounded by green, so wild yet free,
Each day's an adventure, come sit with me.
With laughter and plants, life's quite the scene,
Sheltered by nature, it's a leafy dream!

A Palette of Leaves

In the kitchen where herbs now sway,
Thyme's on the counter, what a display.
Basil plays chef, with a twirl and a spin,
Cooking up laughs, let the basil begin!

The fridge is full of veggies galore,
Their colors burst out, it's a floral store.
Carrots in tutus, potatoes in hats,
What a bizarre dance, done by these spats!

Greens in my smoothies, made to blend fine,
They giggle and gurgle, "We're feeling divine!"
But too many leaves lead to a green scene,
It seems my blender's now part of the green screen.

A palette so vibrant, a feast for my eyes,
Nature's own canvas, where silliness lies.
In this house of green, life's a playful tease,
Filled with laughter and joy, and a hint of peas!

Growing Lullabies within Walls

In corners where the ferns do giggle,
And sunbeams dance a silly wiggle,
We hear the plants hum tunes so sweet,
While vines play tag with little feet.

The pots conspire with whispers low,
To tickle toes and make them glow,
A leafy choir croons with glee,
As if to say, "Come play with me!"

A spider spins a web of cheer,
In this cozy, leafy atmosphere,
Each bloom a joke, each stem a smile,
Their laughter stretches for a mile.

So here we lounge, in shades of green,
Where every leaf is a living meme,
In this sanctuary, joy runs free,
Who knew plants had such a sense of spree?

The Canopy of Heartfelt Shelter

Beneath the branches, we play peek-a-boo,
With squirrels acting out their own review,
The daisies curl up like a soft quilt,
Creating laughter, oh, the joy we've built!

Mossy cushions and dandelion seats,
Where pesky ladybugs rattle their beats,
The air infused with giggling thyme,
Poetic mischief in every rhyme.

Cacti share their prickly jokes,
While tulips giggle at shy little folks,
The breeze teases all in sight,
Come join the fun, it feels so right!

In this leafy abode of jests,
With vines in hats, and flowers as guests,
The shelter wraps us, snug and tight,
In a canopied world, full of delight.

A Nesting Place Among Vines

There's a vine that swings, preparing to fall,
While flowers play dress-up in the hall,
With their bright colors and clumsy moves,
They laugh as they dance to the rhythm that grooves.

The canaries chirp in tones absurd,
As hedgehogs roll on the drowsy herd,
Each petal a smile, each leaf a cheer,
In this nesting place, joy draws near.

Resilient roots tell tales of old,
Of mischief, giggles, and dreams bold,
Trees nod in rhythm, sharing the laughs,
While garden gnomes sit drawing their graphs.

So come and play, don't miss the fun,
In a garden where giggles have just begun,
Each vine a friend, each shrub a jest,
The greenest home, where laughter's blessed!

The Palette of Living Hues

In paint splotches of emerald and jade,
Life bustles on in a leafy parade,
Where bees don tuxedos, all ready to buzz,
And flowers gossip, as only they could.

Chubby caterpillars boast of their size,
While daisies whisper secrets and lies,
The sun-soaked grass chuckles in glee,
As vibrant shades dance, ever so free.

The rainbows spilled from pots and pans,
Create a tapestry only nature plans,
With petals that tickle and branches that tease,
In this crazy canvas, we dance with the breeze!

So grab a brush and let's start to play,
In hues of laughter, we'll blend away,
For in this palette, humor abounds,
Amidst living colors, happiness resounds!

The Swaying Foliage

Leaves dance and twirl, what a sight,
Chasing the wind, oh what a flight.
Squirrels chatter, plotting schemes,
While branches sway, or so it seems.

A breeze tickles all the fronds,
Nature's laughter goes beyond.
Caterpillars munch on leaves,
They think they're kings, if one believes.

Sunshine peeks through, a bright grin,
Shade grows thick, let games begin.
Jumping jacks sold the free air,
Foliage laughter everywhere.

So, if you step beneath the boughs,
Be ready to play, make some vows.
To giggle, scramble, and just be,
Amongst the swaying, leafy spree.

An Arbor's Caress

Underneath the leafy dome,
Where flowers dance, the bees call home.
Pinecones drop, they make a thud,
Watch where you step, or you'll be mud!

Bark's a stage for critters bold,
Telling tales, both funny and old.
A picnic here seems quite a plan,
Until ants decide to stake a claim!

Branches wave like arms in cheer,
"Join us!" they shout, over here!
A hammock swings, too high, too low,
It's like playing tag with the flow.

So if you linger in the shade,
And find a sunbeam that won't fade,
Just laugh with trees that move and sway,
For nature frolics day by day.

Echoes of the Meadow

Green blades tickle my shoelaces,
As I trip through flowered bases.
Bumblebees buzz with endless glee,
While daisies dance and tease me.

In the pond, frogs sing their songs,
"Jump in!" they croak, "Come join along!"
But sticky mud makes me squeal,
A slippery dance, oh what a deal!

Butterflies flutter like confetti,
While ladybugs peek, all so petty.
They roll their eyes as I stumble by,
In this meadow, I try not to cry.

Yet every tumble brings a laugh,
As I chase butterflies on my path.
Tickled by sunbeams and soft breeze,
Life's a jest, filled with such ease!

Green Dreams Abound

In my yard, the herbs play tricks,
Basil whispers, "I'm quite the fix!"
Mint's got jokes, it's full of sass,
While thyme just rolls, hoping to pass.

Ferns look wise, with leafy hair,
Casting shade, like they're the mayor.
"Join the party, don't be shy,"
Said the clover, letting dreams fly high.

Every flower tells a tale,
Petals giggle, breezes sail.
The gnome grins, as he guards the tree,
Hiding secrets, just wait and see!

So if you wander through this plot,
Where dreams are green and laughter's hot,
Join the chatter, the life all round,
In this playful realm where joy is found.

Gentle Echoes in Leafy Corners

In the corner sat a fern,
Whispering tales of why it yearns.
The cat thought it was a new friend,
But it just wanted the nap to extend.

Cacti laugh in spikes of glee,
Telling secrets to the bumblebee.
They claim they hold the best cactus jokes,
But only tell them to prickly folks!

The ivy climbed with great delight,
Inviting all to join the fight.
But all it wanted was to be free,
To swing around like a mischievous tree.

Potting soil's become a dance floor,
With worms practicing moves galore.
They twirl and dip in wiggly bliss,
While the daisies just laugh and reminisce.

The Secret Life of Indoor Gardens

At midnight, the plants hold their shows,
With moonbeams dancing on their toes.
The rosemary's brewing herbal tea,
While mint is plotting a grand jubilee.

Basil dreams of a spicy affair,
With pesto parties beyond compare.
Sage just grins, feeling so wise,
While thyme is always on the rise!

But when the morning sunlight breaks,
They act as if the party's fakes.
Pretending to be all prim and neat,
While under leaves, there's still a beat!

The orchids wink with a polished flair,
Knowing they're the garden's millionaire.
Yet they get jealous of the humble sprout,
Who's stolen hearts without a doubt!

Green Dreams in Every Room

At night, my plants share wild dreams,
Of jungles and sunlit streams.
While I snore, they plot their schemes,
To move around in leafy teams.

The spider plant spins funky sets,
And gets lost in its own pet nets.
The pothos slips to catch some fame,
Trying to become a plant-based game.

Fern flirts with shadows, calm and cool,
While the succulents play it like a fool.
They strut on shelves, the comedians' crew,
Cracking jokes, "Here's one for you!"

When morning comes, they pretend to sleep,
Acting like they've made no leap.
But I know well of their playful spree,
In dreams, they run wild, just like me!

Sweet Serenity Among the Petals

In the garden of dreams, there's laughter and cheer,
With flowers gossiping, spreading good cheer.
Roses argue who's the fairest of all,
While daisies just giggle, too proud to fall.

Tulips strut in their fancy attire,
Displaying colors that inspire.
But sunflowers roll their eyes in jest,
Claiming they're simply the very best!

The violets whisper soft, sweet rhymes,
Counting petals and passing the times.
And lilacs boast about fragrant fun,
While bees buzz in, "We're number one!"

As evening shadows stretch and weave,
The whole bunch gathers to laugh and believe.
In blossoms of magic, a joke takes flight,
Serenity blossoms within the night!

Verdant Whispers of Sanctuary

In the living room, vines dance,
A frog on the shelf steals a glance.
Potted plants gossip, gossip they share,
While daisies wear hats, quite debonair.

The cat is bewildered, what is this place?
With leaves on the ceiling, it's quite the space.
A moss-covered sofa, a cushy delight,
Squirrels throw parties, oh what a sight!

Green curtains flutter, they seem to sigh,
As the parakeet lectures on how to fly.
"Stay grounded!" they yell, "or you'll hit the fan!"
Yet they all laugh, for they're part of the plan.

Murals of forests, a whimsical dream,
Where snails wear shoes—oh, what a team!
Each corner a tale, charming and zany,
In this leafy abode, life's never brainy.

Emerald Embrace of Hearth

The kitchen you see, overgrown with cheer,
A cucumber wears glasses, oh dear, oh dear!
The fridge murmurs secrets of herbs gone wild,
While the thyme pokes fun, it's nature's mild child.

Mint leaves hold court in a pot with a grin,
"Who's ready for tea? Let the fun begin!"
Even the rice laughs, "I'm boiled with glee!"
In this tangled kingdom, all's joyful and free.

A chair made of ferns proudly stands,
While the dog snoozes, dreaming of bands.
Lettuce serenades the old, dusty broom,
In this vibrant space, there's always more room.

Basil leads yoga, quite flexible, see?
"Downward Dog, everyone, with the flea!"
A parsley parade gets the party begun,
In this sea of green, there's laughter and fun.

Lush Corners of Comfort

In cozy nooks, ferns drape like a shawl,
While roses compete for the title of tall.
The rabbit in plaid holds court with the cats,
In a world where no one wears silly hats!

Caladiums chatter, their colors a riot,
While petunias gossip, "Did you see that diet?"
The sofa's a jungle, the cushions a mess,
With leaves growing thick, it's quite the success!

In this jungle den where no one is shy,
Lettuce plays poker while the chives say, "Hi!"
Everyone's playing, it's never too late,
With giggles and mischief that percolate.

As dusk settles down, the fireflies come,
A chorus of giggles, a green drum drum.
Nature's big joke, with each turn of a leaf,
In laughter and whimsy, we find our belief.

Nature's Cradle of Serenity

Bamboo whispers softly, a secretive sound,
While the orchids giggle, up in their crown.
Goldfish swim by, tossing popcorn like dreams,
In a world where water dances and gleams.

The hallway is lined with plants on the run,
A cactus in shades says, "Oh, this is fun!"
Petals jump high with a skip and a hop,
In playful confusion, they never will stop.

A potted parade, all lined in a row,
Ferns sing of futures where fun always flows.
While daffodils chatter, "We're blooming with pride!"
And in this butterfly palace, joys coincide.

So come take a look, in laughter we roam,
In this bucolic, green, riotous home.
It's a whimsical world where nature's the key,
Unlocking the joys of pure jubilee!

The Glow of the Garden

In the backyard, a gnome dozed,
Clad in moss like an old man's clothes.
He dreamed of racing with the blooms,
While ladybugs plotted in the rooms.

A scarecrow pranced—a jig he tried,
With crows all laughing, they nearly cried.
He danced among the daisies bright,
But tripped on a weed, oh what a sight!

Lettuce whispers secrets to the sun,
I swear they giggle; gardening's fun!
Tomatoes blush while the radishes peek,
It's a veggie party, all week, all week!

The daisies gossip, oh how they thrive,
With bees as bouncers, keeping it alive.
In this wild patch, mischief is grand,
Nature's kooky circus, oh isn't it planned!

Soft Shadows and Leafy Light

Underneath the willow, critters play,
The shadows dance in a mischievous way.
A squirrel in sunglasses, quite the sight,
Stealing acorns, gleeful delight!

The grass tickles toes, what a pesky tease,
As butterflies flutter on the warm breeze.
A worm in a bow tie, ready to chat,
'I'm formal today! How about that?'

The daisies play tag with the buzzing bees,
Each petal a giggle, each stem with ease.
Through sunbeams they race, no rules apply,
While the old oak just shakes his head and sighs.

In this leafy realm, the fun never ends,
With roots in the ground, and hearts like friends.
Each leaf a laugh, each flower a cheer,
In this garden party, all are welcome here!

A Symphony of Blooms

The roses croon in a fragrant choir,
While tulips tap dance, never tire.
With petals and leaves, they make quite the show,
A riotous concert, oh look at them go!

The bees are the conductors, buzzing away,
While crickets play drums at the end of the day.
The daisies on backup, they're ready to hum,
As butterflies waltz, oh the fun has begun!

A sunbeam's a spotlight, a warm golden glow,
On this stage of the flora, the performance will flow.
In the midst of the fun, a garden cat grins,
As petals all flutter, let the show begin!

Ode to the soil, and the creatures that dwell,
Each bloom tells a story, and oh what a swell!
So join in the laughter, come dance on the green,
In the symphony of nature, we're free and serene!

Cradled by Verdure

In the embrace of the leafy arms,
A squirrel plots with his charming charms.
He claims the oak tree as his own throne,
While debating with snails who are never alone.

The ferns giggle, whispering smack,
As the garden hedgehog prepares to attack.
With a roll and a dart, what a ruckus in sight,
As the tulips gasp, oh what a fright!

A rabbit in sneakers runs wild and free,
Chasing a butterfly, 'Catch me if you can!' you see.
With a hop and a skip, he twirls in delight,
While the daisies clap, oh, what a night!

Nestled in laughter, rooted in glee,
Nature's own stage, what a merry spree!
With rustling leaves and a breeze that's funky,
Here in the greenery, life's never chunky!

Depths of the Glade

In the shade where weeds do sprout,
A rabbit hops, he gives a shout.
The gnome's hat's lost, it rolled away,
He'll find it here, just not today.

A turtle strolls, he's on a quest,
Swinging his head, he's quite the jest.
The snail has won the slowest race,
While daisies giggle, a flowery lace.

The breeze tickles leaves, making them dance,
As squirrels plot their next nutty chance.
A frog sings opera by the old pond,
The crickets clap, they're quite the fond.

In this glade of eternal cheer,
Laughter echoes, life's veneer.
The whispers of nature, a comic delight,
In this green stage, everything feels right.

Joy in the Leafy Bower

Under the arch of twisting vines,
The parrots gossip, sipping wines.
A beehive party, buzzing with glee,
While flowers gossip, 'Oh look at me!'

A raccoon wears shades, struts with flair,
Proclaims his fashion beyond compare.
The mushrooms dance, their cap so spry,
In this leafy bower, all are awry.

Treetop swings made from old twine,
Monkeys laughing, sipping on brine.
They're making trouble, a slippery mess,
But in this chaos, there's no stress.

So come take part in this leafy fun,
Chaos guaranteed, no need to run.
Amidst the green, every heart is light,
In this joyful world, the mood is bright.

The Essences of Earth

In the soil where secrets dwell,
Worms play tag, and they do well.
With a wiggle and jiggle, they roll about,
Announcing to all, 'We're the best clout!'

A bug parade, with tiny bands,
Dancing to rhythms, in nature's lands.
These critters don't care about the grime,
Their world's a party, all the time.

A tree's old trunk wears a wise old grin,
While fungi sprout, laughing within.
In the essence of earth, joy is found,
Among playful critters, all around.

So embrace the magic of this funny place,
Where nonsense blooms and smiles interlace.
With every leaf, the laughter expands,
In this world of green, humor commands.

Spaces of Renewal

In a nook where the daffodils bloom,
A squirrel's made a dusty room.
He claims it's cozy, but I disagree,
With acorns stacked in chaotic spree.

The compost heap has become a stage,
As critters come forth, to earn their wage.
They tell their tales with such flair,
Of how they dodge, in the compost air.

A scarecrow's hat flies off in the breeze,
While birds are laughing, doing as they please.
They're practicing lines for their next big show,
In these spaces of green, there's much to know.

So let's renew our spirit with fun,
In this green playground, we all can run.
Life's just better with a giggle or two,
In spaces reborn, there's always a view.

Embracing Nature's Palette

In the garden, weeds do dance,
With a twirl and a cheeky prance.
They wear a crown of colors bright,
And say, 'Who needs to mow tonight?'

The daisies joke with the bumblebees,
Trading secrets in the gentle breeze.
'You think you're sweet?' the lilacs tease,
'But I'm the one that brings them to their knees!'

Grasshoppers hop like they own the place,
With tiny sunglasses and swaggered grace.
'Why work so hard, oh human friend?
Just chill with us until the day's end!'

The tomatoes grin, ripe and bold,
With stories of sunshine and joy untold.
As we sip lemonade, laughter in the air,
Nature's humor, a gift so rare.

Whispers of Wildflowers

In a field where wildflowers bloom,
They conspire to steal all the room.
'I'm the most colorful!' the poppy shouts,
While the daisies roll their eyes with doubts.

The sunflowers stand, tall and proud,
Trying to be the life of the crowd.
'Look at me, I'm reaching high!'
But forget to wave to the butterflies nearby.

'Caution!' cries the clover, 'Step with care!'
'You might trip over my heartfelt flair.'
Just then a squirrel drops a nut,
And everyone giggles at the sudden strut.

As bees buzz by with a busy tune,
They laugh at the flowers, saying, 'Oh, you'll swoon!'
While clover just chuckles, ever so sly,
'You know, I'm low-key, but I still fly high!'

A Celebration of Growth

In the corner, a cactus jokes,
'Wish I could wear some fancy cloaks!'
While the ferns, all frilly and lush,
Say, 'We frolic; you just sit and hush!'

Bamboo sticks together, bending low,
'Look at me flexing, stealing the show!'
But the tulips in bloom laugh and sing,
'Bamboo, darling, quit imagining!'

The carrots underground plot their rise,
'We'll be the stars, oh what a surprise!'
And the radishes giggle, all red and round,
'Might take a while, but we'll astound!'

In this wild medley, joy takes root,
With every wink of a leaf or a shoot.
Nature's humor, a merry affair,
Sprouting laughter, everywhere!

Swaying Under the Canopy

Under the trees, the shadows play,
The acorns whisper, 'Join the ballet!'
Branches sway as the wind comes by,
'We're the cool kids,' they chuckle and sigh.

The oak boasts of age, wisdom profound,
While the saplings giggle, jumping around.
'Age is just bark, nothing more!'
Says a breeze that flirts with the forest floor.

'Watch out for squirrels on a nutty spree!'
Cried the pine with glee, 'They've made a decree!'
Fluffy-tailed, they leap and they bound,
Each landing with laughter that echoes around.

As twilight falls, the fireflies spark,
Lighting up tales in the softening dark.
Under this canopy, giggles abound,
In the laughter of nature, joy is found.

The Abundance of Leaves

In the corner, a plant grows tall,
It thinks it's winning the leaf-giving ball.
Each leaf that drops, it counts with glee,
As if it's gathering gold for a spree.

The little cactus is feeling quite proud,
With needles so sharp, it shouts out loud.
'I'm hardy!', it brags, 'I need no rain!'
While succulents giggle, 'Just wait for your pain!'

Ferns do a dance, swaying with grace,
They whisper secrets, take up some space.
"I'm the favorite!" they whisper and tease,
While all the flowers are begging, "Please!"

But when autumn rolls and things turn gray,
The leaves all flutter, then drift away.
"Oh no!" cries the plant, "Where'd everyone go?"
"Just wait for spring, you'll have quite the show!"

The Murmurs of Chlorophyll

Beneath the sun, a leaf starts to talk,
It's gossiping gently, like a sly hawk.
"Did you see how that shrub pruned its bush?
Talk about drama, oh what a rush!"

The daisies snicker, their petals aflame,
"Did you hear? That rose thinks it's the same!"
With thorns for protection, it puffs out its chest,
But inside, it knows it's just like the rest.

The ivy climbs higher, it yearns for the sky,
While the fern rolls its eyes, wondering why.
A meeting is called, as the weeds start to scheme,
"Let's take down the tulips, it's time to redeem!"

But when the gardener comes with a pruner in hand,
All whispers hush, they can't make a stand.
"Not us, we're innocent!" they all start to plead,
As they laugh and wiggle, refusing to heed!

Fragrance of the Garden

The roses smell sweet, they wear such a crown,
While daisies insist that they'll never frown.
In a mix of scents, the garden's a show,
By the fence, there's a whiff from a sneaky tomato.

Marigolds giggle; they're striking a pose,
"Look at us, bright! We're the stars of the rows!"
But potatoes underground, they just shake their heads,
"We're the true heroes, without any beds!"

The herbs join the fun, with a pungent delight,
"Basil's our name, and we dance every night!"
But mint rolls its eyes, and with a sly swoosh,
"I'm the coolest around!" it giggles and whoosh!

Yet when humans walk in with fingers for snipping,
The plants all their banter start hastily flipping.
"Not me!" they all shout, as they brace for the cut,
While the weeds in the corner just snicker and strut!

The Allure of Greenery

A jungle of plants, a party at night,
The mosses are dancing, it's quite a sight.
They throw a bash, with roots intertwined,
"Don't mind us, we're just getting aligned!"

The ferns flutter wildly, their wings aglow,
While the herbs add a dab of fragrant show.
"It's all about smell!" they boastfully chime,
But the grass on the ground just shrugs, "We're fine!"

The tulips roll by, wearing colorful hats,
They strut with pride, giving sass to the cats.
"Oh, do take a look at our fabulous hue,
We're the life of the garden, we're more than a view!"

Yet when the sun sets and darkness is near,
All chatter subsides, just whispers appear.
"Until next time," a daisy softly beams,
"In the world of greenery, we live in our dreams!"

A Retreat in Foliage

In my house of leafy dreams,
I've got more plants than beams.
They grow and stretch, it's quite a feat,
Sometimes I trip on roots in my fleet.

The cactus waves, it likes to poke,
While ferns gossip about my joke.
My spider plant hungers for sun,
So I laid out a solar run.

With vines that climb and never rest,
I'm convinced they think they're the best.
I painted them with funny smiles,
Now they cheer my awkward styles.

So here amongst these verdant friends,
Life's like a game that never ends.
We laugh and play through each green season,
Who knew plants could have such a reason?

Growing with Nature

The spinach whispers, 'I'm a star!'
While tomatoes argue, 'We're bizarre!'
Each sprout has dreams of grandeur bright,
But usually just leaves for my bite.

The basil's had too much to think,
Doing yoga, sipping on a drink.
Mint told a joke, but it's too minty,
It's fresh and funny, but a tad chintzy.

When carrots hide beneath the ground,
They chuckle softly, not making a sound.
They know the secret, never to show,
That growing takes time and seeds must sow.

So here I stand, my plants all around,
With leaves that dance to nature's sound.
In this garden, nothing feels wrong,
We grow together, where we belong.

Tides of Green

Waves of lettuce sway and sway,
While sprouts have come out to play.
In this sea of emerald delight,
I paddle through, what a sight!

The kale tries to build a raft,
While my radishes crack a draft.
They joke about their leafy might,
Saying, 'Who needs a boat for flight?'

The broccoli shouts, 'We're top crew!'
As the peas roll by in a wild view.
We surf on vines, oh what a scene!
Just don't fall into the frothy green!

Every wave brings laughter anew,
In this garden, fun's for the few.
With laughter and veggies side by side,
Tides of green, let's enjoy the ride!

Nestled in Nature's Hues

In a nook of life, where colors burst,
Chlorophyll dreams are truly cursed.
The daisies giggle, the daisies trip,
I'm their audience on this fun trip.

A squirrel runs by in a frantic dash,
Chasing a nut, oh what a clash!
The daisies cheer, 'You can do it!'
While the oak quips, 'You really blew it!'

In the meadow, odd tales unfold,
Even the mushrooms have stories bold.
They whisper secrets from the ground,
Each one full of laughs that abound.

So here I am, in shades so bright,
With nature's quirks that feel just right.
Together we blend, a quirky crew,
In this silly garden, forever true.

The Secret Garden Within

In my backyard, there's quite a scene,
A patch of jungle where none has been.
The neighbors peek over, they cough and they stare,
Wondering if Tarzan might swing from a chair.

I plant a tomato, it grows like a vine,
It's taken my patio, it's crossed every line.
The squirrels hold a party, it's their new buffet,
They've welcomed my veggies, come what may!

My flowers are wild, with colors that clash,
A rainbow explosion, a haphazard splash.
But the bees keep on buzzing, they throw quite a fit,
Saying, "Dude, pick a color! We need a committee!"

At dusk I sit back, with a cup in my hand,
And watch as my weeds do a funky dance stand.
They twist and they twirl, in the bright moonlight,
It's a backyard rave and I'm feeling just right!

Where Nature Blooms

In the corner of my kitchen, there's a plant in a pot,
It's thriving so well, I'm impressed, I'm not hot.
It just sits there grinning, while I'm in despair,
How can it be thriving, when I can't comb my hair?

A cactus on my windowsill sharpens its spikes,
I'm convinced it's plotting for future bike hikes.
While I'm busy drinking my green smoothie blend,
It nods approvingly, saying, "You're my friend!"

The daisies in the garden are laughing so loud,
With petals that shake, they're taking a bow.
"Look at us, humans, we bloom without care!"
I argue back softly, "But we don't have air!"

The squirrels start rehearsing their newest ballet,
They're pirouetting freely; it's a sly little play.
Nature plays tricks, it tickles my soul,
In this world of greenery, I've found my goal!

Living with Flora

I share my abode with a leafy brigade,
They feast on my leftovers, and never are swayed.
They plot on my counter, my cilantro's a spy,
I swear it reports to the chives by and by.

The basil holds council with thyme on a chair,
Arguing loudly about who has the flair.
While the lettuce lounges, it really looks grand,
Its dreams of becoming a souffle are unplanned!

In the hallway, my ferns grow taller each day,
I swear they're just showing off in a green ballet.
They wave to the curtains, give high-fives to chairs,
It's a home for organisms, with funny affairs!

So as I trip over a vine with a sigh,
The petunias look up with a twinkle, "Oh my!
Impromptu jungle, we thrive with such glee,
Just one little mishap, and you'll bloom like a tree!"

Corners of Cleansing Green

In the smallest nook, a fern starts to grow,
Inhibiting my space, it's putting on a show.
I think it's rehearsing for some ferny play,
While I'm just hoping it'll stay out of the way.

The mint in the pot has become quite a beast,
It shows off its leaves like a fresh herbal feast.
As I reach for my tea, it lashes out in glee,
"Just a sprig for you, but I'm more than a tree!"

A jade plant chats gossip with lavender sprigs,
While the succulents snicker, "We're way more big!"
It's a botanical planet, with drama to boot,
And I, the unwitting, am stuck in a root!

In the corners of green, life's laughter does dwell,
Each leaf brings a chuckle, a story to tell.
My friends may be plants, but they really do shine,
For living with greenery is simply divine!

The Scent of Earthy Respite

In the corner, a plant gobbles light,
Not sure if it's hungry or just polite.
The cat sits still, plotting a heist,
Napping, dreaming of leaves over rice.

There's a cactus with pride, so sharp and stout,
It pokes at the door to chase folks out.
Yet the flowers nearby, so vibrant and bright,
Gossip all day, till the fall of night.

A gnome in a chair, sipping plant-based tea,
Claims the daisies have better company.
But when I look close, in a twist of fate,
They're whispering secrets, deciding his fate.

And when rain drizzles down, it's quite the sight,
The veggies dance salsa, what a delight!
With greens that sprout laughter, oh what a scene,
This place is alive, and oh so obscene.

Leafy Abode of Tranquility

The ivy creeps up, a curious guest,
Snooping on conversations, that's not its best.
While ferns and fronds throw a wild soiree,
The dog thinks it's time to join in the play.

Pots bump and clatter, the spoons all align,
Mint is making drinks, while thyme draws the line.
A chili pepper is feeling quite hot,
Mixing up gossip, plotting a plot.

The windows all shuffle, as butterflies flit,
Chatting with daisies, they won't have to sit.
While the sun peeks in, the shadows do dance,
Even the pumpkins are joining the prance!

An owl on a branch takes a break from the show,
Sipping on wisdom, with nowhere to go.
Laughter erupts from the lettuce brigade,
In this leafy abode, who needs a parade?

Garden of Forgotten Dreams

In the soil lie secrets of what could have been,
Rubber boots murmur tales of all the green.
Once a daisy dreamed, 'I could fly to the moon!',
Now just sways gently to the sound of a tune.

Radishes sing songs of the things lost to time,
With carrots composing a vegetable rhyme.
A wilted old rose, with stories untold,
Winks at the chill of the air growing cold.

The squirrels hold court under the old oak's shade,
Discussing acorns and the mix-up they made.
While worms in the dirt delight in their quest,
Building little castles, oh, aren't they blessed?

Overgrown herbs compete for the limelight,
Basil says, "Dill, you've got to take flight!"
But rosemary laughs, "Not on my watch!"
In this garden of dreams, it's quite the balmy swatch.

Where Ferns Find Solace

In a corner, the ferns gather for tea,
Pipping and chatting, oh, what jubilee!
Sipping on dew drops, they gossip and jest,
With potting soil stories, they consider the best.

A snail, the slowpoke, is late to the show,
Promises made of races all in the flow.
While mushrooms insist they have magic in store,
They giggle and prance like they're never a bore.

The sun sets low, painting smiles on each leaf,
Tickling the roots, a moment of relief.
As shadows grow longer, the ferns start to sway,
Whispering secrets, till the light fades away.

And in this forest of laughter and fun,
Every plant knows it's just begun.
So follow the laughter, let joy take the lead,
For where ferns find solace, there's always a need!

www.ingramcontent.com/pod-product-compliance
Lightning Source LLC
Chambersburg PA
CBHW070313120526
44590CB00017B/2663